On line with God

At last! practical help with how to pray

David Lawrence

Scripture Union

one up

B O O K S

© David Lawrence 1997
First published 1997
Reprinted 1998

Scripture Union, 207–209
Queensway, Bletchley, Milton Keynes,
MK2 2EB, England.

ISBN 1 85999 185 8

British Library Cataloguing-in-
Publication Data.
A catalogue record of this book is
available from the British Library.

Printed and bound in Great Britain by
Ebenezer Baylis & Sons Ltd,
Worcester.

All the song excerpts on the
accompanying CD have been
recorded by the *World Wide
Message Tribe* and are used by kind
permission of Movation/Alliance
Records.

Design and illustration:
Wild Associates

Photography: Matt Harris

Scripture Union

Making the connection

Doddy Doodwell was frustrated.

He'd had an electric guitar and amplifier for his birthday but it didn't seem to work. He looked down at the bright red Fender Stratocaster slung around his neck and retwiddled the volume and tone controls before giving it another strum. The barely audible jangling of the steel strings caused Doddy to sigh and turn his attention to the amplifier. He spoke to himself as he checked it, 'Plug? In. Power button? On. Volume control? Maximum. Should be enough noise coming out of this thing to bring the roof caving in! What is wrong with you?'

The amplifier wasn't letting on.

Doddy's sister Desdemelza entered the room.

'Come on then, Oh Big-Brother-Mega-Star of mine. Play us a song.'

Doddy looked annoyed at this interruption.

'Push off, Dessy. I don't need you and your smart comments at the moment, thank you. This thing's not working; I think Mum will have to take it back to the shop.'

Desdemelza Doodwell was not famous for either her musical or technical know-how but she ventured to ask, 'Have you plugged in the amplifier?'

'Of course!'

'Have you turned it on?'

'Do you think I'm stupid?'

Desdemelza wisely chose not to answer that question but risking her brother's wrath she ventured to ask, 'Have you checked the lead?'

'What?'

Desdemelza repeated, 'Have you checked the lead? You know, the wire that takes the sound from your guitar into the amplifier!'

As it happened, Doddy had not checked the lead. He grasped the bright green cable where it joined his guitar and gave the connector a wiggle. All secure at that end so he ran his hand along the length of the cable to where it disappeared to the connecting socket on the back of the amplifier. As he pulled the cable the trailing end appeared from behind his amplifier and swung limply from his fingers. He shot a warning look at Desmedelza: 'Pretend you haven't seen this', it said. But it was too late.

Through tears of near-helpless laughter, Desdemelza made it quite clear that she had seen all. 'You Grade one heavy-duty bone-headed BOZO!' she shrieked in delight. 'This doesn't work. Mum will have to take it back,' she mimicked mercilessly.

As she spoke, Doddy plugged in the offending lead and without readjusting any of the controls gave the strings an almighty twang.

Desdemelza was still laughing as the ceiling fell on her head.

Trying to play an electric guitar without making the connection to the amplifier is a bit like trying to be a Christian without making regular prayer-connections to God. In both cases the lack of a good connection means a total loss of power!

You may have seen the poster:

SEVEN DAYS WITHOUT PRAYER MAKE ONE WEAK!

It's true! If we don't make space in our lives for plugging into God then we will end up spiritually weak and consequently unable to know or serve him as we should.

JESUS had a lot to teach his followers about prayer. Here's one of the things that he taught: 'When you pray, go to your room, close the door, and pray to your Father, who is unseen. And your Father, who sees what you do in private, will reward you.' (Matthew 6:6)

According to Jesus, God wants us to take time out just to talk to him. Think about that for a moment! The most *awesome* being in the Universe, the great *Creator* of stars and planets (not to mention cute fluffy little bunnies!) invites you to call him 'Father' and drop in for a one-on-one chat *every day*. It would be a staggering thing to have that privilege once in a lifetime but to have it any time, every day is almost beyond belief.

And yet isn't it amazing that we often turn down the invitation because we're too busy, or too tired... or we just don't think it's important!!

Let's get our heads into gear and recognise that personal prayer is not only a privilege but crucial to growing as a Christian. No-one pretends that it is always easy so this book is written for people who want to pray but find it hard. If you follow the guidelines in this book you will gradually find prayer easier and as you make the connection with God, he will see, hear and answer. Try it!!

How to use this book

Before going any further just take some time out to get acquainted with the book that is in your hands. Here's the menu:

- MAKING THE CONNECTION
- GETTING STARTED
- INTRODUCING...
- ... PRAYER LOG
- PRAYER FILES
- ... REVISITED
- PRAYER-AID
- PEOPLE WHO PRAYED
- PRAYER GRAPHICS
- PRAYER CD

MAKING THE CONNECTION

(p3,4) If you're not yet sure that prayer is important, read this!

GETTING STARTED

(p7) Three practical steps for getting going.

INTRODUCING...

... PRAYER LOG

The main part of this book is a thirteen-week prayer guide. Over the thirteen weeks you will be helped to pray in the following six ways:

Telling God what he means to you
Telling God you're sorry
Telling God you're grateful
Asking God for what you need
Asking God for what others need
Listening to God

Each section has a double-page introduction followed by two weeks of **Prayer Log** (see pages 8–13 for example).

Prayer Logs give you the basic framework for your daily prayer time. There is also a **Prayer Web-site** on each **Prayer Log** page so that you can chart your progress as you work through the book.

As each week goes by you will have to spend slightly longer to complete the day's task. Don't worry that at first you may only be spending 2 or 3 minutes a day in prayer. By the end of the booklet you will want to be face to face with God for about 20 minutes (although you could take a lot longer if you liked!).

The amount of time spent is not the most important factor. The vital thing is that you spend long enough to know that you are focusing in on God and making the connection.

Have a good look at the Prayer Log pages (eg p10,11) and at the Prayer Webs so that you understand how to use them when you get to them.

PRAYER FILES

Written prayers on different themes all ready for you to use when you run out of your own words (eg p30).

PEOPLE WHO PRAYED

Real-life examples of the difference that prayer can make (p32,47)!

... REVISITED

A fresh look at a previous week's prayer theme to remind you of where you've been!

PRAYER GRAPHICS

The colour pictures at the centre of the book will form a part of your prayer times (we'll tell you when!).

PRAYER-AID

Various articles scattered throughout the book looking at questions like 'Who Am I Talking To?' (p15), 'How To Pray With Faith' (p37) and 'Why Doesn't God Answer My Prayers?' (p46).

PRAYER CD

The CD on the cover of this book is not just a freebie promo! As the weeks go by, you will be directed to use different tracks from the CD in your prayer times. If you haven't got a CD player perhaps you could get a friend to copy the songs onto a tape for you.

Getting started

Before launching in to **Prayer Log Week 1**, you need to do the following three things:

1 Decide on your prayer space

Where are you going to get together with God? It needs to be a place where you can be alone and uninterrupted. Most young people use their bedroom as their prayer space. If you share your bedroom with a brother or sister, negotiate a time when you can have the room to yourself for about twenty minutes.

Make a notice to hang outside your prayer room when you are praying, eg 'Important meeting in progress: Do not disturb!'

Make a note of your prayer space here:
My prayer space is in *My Lounge.*

2 Decide on your prayer time

Fixing a time when you are going to try to pray each day is vital. Of course God is with us all the time, but the kind of focused prayer-appointment that we are talking about in this book will not just 'happen'. It needs to be planned and the arrangements need to be kept to.

Most young people who pray regularly do so at night before going to bed and this book assumes that you will do that too. However, don't leave it too late so that you give God the bit of the day when you feel too exhausted to concentrate. It may be better to carve a bit of time out of the early part of the evening rather than wait until you can't keep your eyes open.

If you want to use a different part of the day – that's fine – the book will still work for you.

Whether you choose early, middle or late in the day, decide a definite time in your mind and do all that you can to stick to it. If after a week or two it's not working out, then review it and try a different time of day.

Make a note of your prayer time here: *8.00*
I am going to try to pray at each day. *in the evening*

3 Copy the CD onto tape

Of course, you may have a CD player in your prayer space but if not, you will need to have a copy on tape to play in your Walkman. (Maybe someone at church could do it for you if you haven't got a CD player at home.)

GOD
– YOU'RE AWESOME

[telling God what he means to you]

> *Dear God,*
> *please could you fix it for my mum to get less stressy,*
> *my teachers to set less homework, my brother to*
> *forget that I owe him five quid and for Darren Barron*
> *to forget where I live. Please, please, please answer*
> *(especially the bit about my teachers).*
> *Amen.*

For many people prayer is simply presenting a list of problems to God. It is a good thing to ask God to help us out of tight spots but rather than focus on our problems, the first thing that we should do when we start to pray is to focus our minds on God.

In the busy-ness and hassle of a day, God can easily get shoved to the sidelines of our minds and become kind of small in our thinking.

When we start to pray we need to bring God back from the sidelines into the centre of the pitch. We need to make him big again in our thoughts so that when we move on to ask for his help we know we're talking to a big God who can answer our prayers.

Perhaps the best way to do this is to spend a few minutes actually worshipping God as we start to pray.

Worship is simply reminding ourselves of how great God is and then telling him that we reckon he's awesomely wonderful. It is telling and showing God that he is worth a lot to us (it is quite literally 'worth-ship'!).

introducing

But you might have had a bad week. The cat might have eaten the budgie or the ceiling may have fallen on your sister's head. How can you worship God then? Here are some of the reasons the Bible gives for worshipping God – and they are all true, whatever sort of week we are having:

- because he created a beautiful world for us to live in;
- because he has promised us hope for the future;
- because he is *the* greatest being in the universe;
- because he loves us – no matter what;
- because he forgives us when we mess up (again!).

So our first steps in prayer are going to be worship steps!

What To Do Each Day   weeks 1+2

1   Over the next two weeks you will be asked to spend four or five minutes each day simply worshipping God in your prayer space at your prayer time.

2   When you first settle down to start, *do not* rush straight into the day's worship activity. Take a couple of minutes to be quiet and *chill out*; just sit still and quiet, take your mind off what you've just been doing and focus it onto God.

3   The instructions for each day are printed in full on the *Prayer Log* pages that follow.

4   Each day, as you read the suggested verses or listen to the songs on the CD, really try to picture yourself in God's presence and make the words of the readings or songs your own.

You might like to repeat them several times because often it takes a few times through to feel that we really are actually making the connection to God.

5   You might also find it helpful to experiment with different body positions to express your worship (see *God you're awesome – revisited*, p23).

Entering God's presence through worship makes prayer much easier – like getting the focus right on your camera before taking the pictures. So spend the next couple of weeks learning to be a worshipper and you're well on the way to becoming a pray-er!

Come, let us praise the Lord! ...
For the Lord is a mighty God.

Psalm 95:1,3

Sunday:
Psalm 100 says, 'Worship the Lord with JOY; come before him with happy songs!' Close your eyes and picture yourself in a happy crowd surrounding God on his throne. Play track 1 from the CD – 'Hosanna' – and join in with the song to praise God. Play it more than once.

Monday:
Listen to track 2 from the CD – 'I believe in Jesus'. It describes Jesus as the Son of God who died and rose again for us and reminds us that he is near us to help us and forgive us. When the music finishes, choose and use one of the prayers from the **Prayer File** on page 14.

Tuesday:
Open your Bible to Psalm 145:1–3. Listen to track 3 from the CD – 'Jesus, name above all names'. When it has finished, slowly read the verses from Psalm 145 as your own words of worship to Jesus.

Wednesday:
Worship Jesus today using track 4 from the CD – 'All heaven declares'. You will find the words in **Prayer File 1** on page 14.
When the song has finished, use your own words to tell Jesus how great you think he is.

Thursday:
Read Psalm 145:7-9. Write some of the things that are said about God here (eg 'He is good', 'He is kind' etc): _He is righteous_
He is gracious. He is compassionate
He is merciful, He is slow to anger
Use your own words to praise God for what he is like!

Friday:
'Holy, holy, holy! The Lord Almighty is HOLY!' (Isaiah 6:3). God is magnificently awesomely wonderful! Close your eyes, picture yourself in God's presence and listen to track 5 from the CD – 'Holy'.

Saturday:
Take a long look at the picture of Jesus on the cross on page 33. Isn't it marvellous that Jesus loved us enough to die for us? Use your own words to praise him!

prayer log

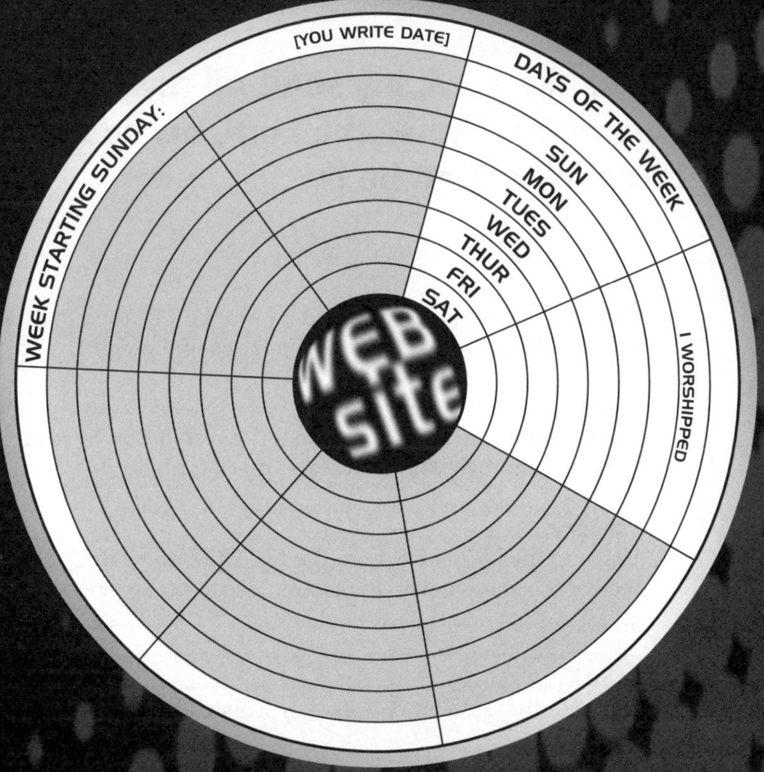

WEEK STARTING SUNDAY:

[YOU WRITE DATE]

DAYS OF THE WEEK

SUN
MON
TUES
WED
THUR
FRI
SAT

web site

I WORSHIPPED

prayer log I web site

For instructions about what to do this week read pages 8 and 9 carefully.

Don't forget to chill out before starting to worship by sitting still and quiet for a few moments. This will help you to refocus your mind on the job in hand – talking to God.

Shade in the appropriate space in the *Prayer Web* above to indicate which days you worshipped this week.

prayer *log*

Praise the Lord, my soul! All my being, praise his holy name! Praise the Lord, my soul, and do not forget how kind he is.

Psalm 103:1,2

Sunday:
Worship God using tracks 1 and 2 from the CD. Then use a prayer from the **Prayer File** on page 14 to worship him some more!

Monday:
Psalm 104 is one long 'praise poem'. Worship God by reading it out aloud to him, as though you had written it just for him!

Tuesday:
Listen to tracks 2 and 3 from the CD. Write down three statements about Jesus each starting with the words 'Jesus, you are special to me because...'

....

....

Use your three statements as your worship prayers today.

Wednesday:
If you haven't experimented with different body positions yet (p23), for today's worship kneel down and picture yourself kneeling in front of Jesus. As you kneel, listen to track 3 from the CD then join in with track 4 (words on page 14).

Thursday:
Take a long look at the 'Creation' picture on page 35. Read Psalm 8 to God as though it was your own poem of praise!

Friday:
Write your own simple worship prayer to Jesus here:
'Jesus I want to worship you today because...'

....

....

Saturday:
Use the first five tracks of the CD to worship God today. Try a different body position for each track, eg Track 1: Stomp around. Track 2: Stand still. Track 3: Sit. Track 4: Kneel. Track 5: Bow down to the floor.

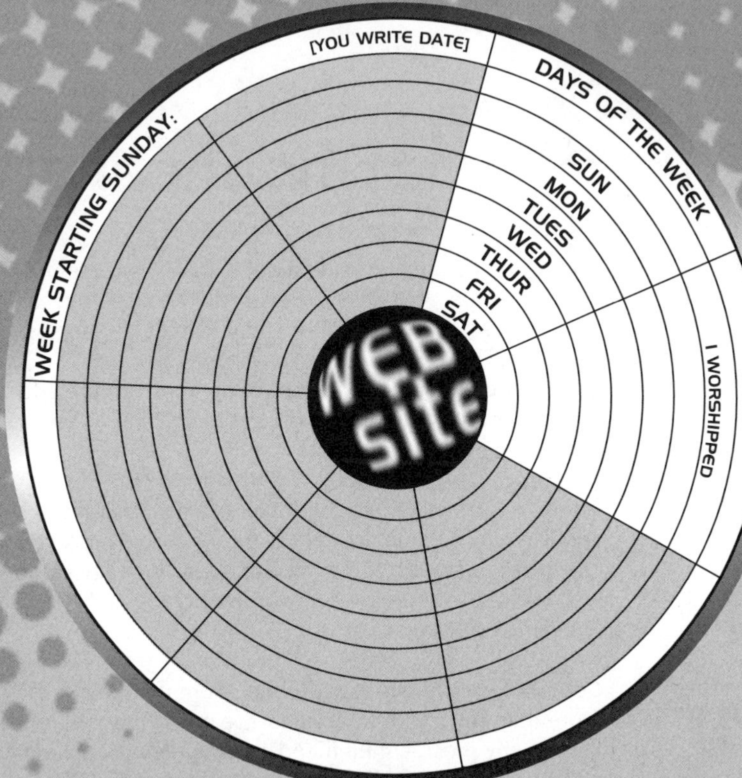
[YOU WRITE DATE]
DAYS OF THE WEEK
WEEK STARTING SUNDAY:
SUN
MON
TUES
WED
THUR
FRI
SAT
I WORSHIPPED
WEB site

prayer log 2 web site

When you don't *feel* like worshipping God, do it anyway! Psalm 103:1,2 (see the top of facing page) encourages us to talk to ourselves (it's not always a sign of madness!!). If your feelings are saying, 'We don't want to worship God today', then speak right back at them and say, 'God is good and kind so I am going to praise him whether you like it or not!!'

Don't forget to shade in the *Prayer Web* to show which days you worshipped this week!

If you miss a day, don't panic! Every day is a chance to start again.

Telling God
what he means to you

God, when I stop and think about how *big* you are my mind just can't cope. A God who is powerful enough to create the universe, vast enough to fill it and intelligent enough to design our incredible world is *awesome* beyond understanding. In the quietness of my room, at the end of the day I bow before you and want to say that as far as I'm concerned, 'You're the greatest!'

Father in heaven, I'm amazed that you should want to stop and listen to me and yet I know that you do. Thank you for caring about me. I stand in awe of a God who knows me so well and yet is willing to accept me so completely. You are wonderful and I worship you.

God, you're worth so much to me. More than my music collection, more than my favourite designer-wear and more than my friends. You are my most faithful friend and your love is my most special possession. May you be just as mega in the morning!

All heaven declares the glory of the risen Lord.
Who can compare with the beauty of the Lord?
For ever he will be the Lamb upon the throne;
I gladly bow the knee and worship him alone.

I will proclaim the glory of the risen Lord
Who once was slain to reconcile man to God.
For ever you will be the Lamb upon the throne;
I gladly bow the knee and worship you alone.
Tricia Richards © Thank You Music

I will proclaim your greatness my God and king;
I will thank you for ever and ever.
Every day I will thank you;
I will praise you for ever and ever.
You Lord are great and you deserve to be HIGHLY praised;
Your greatness is beyond understanding!
(from Psalm 145:1-3, adapted)

prayer file

Who am I talking to ?

Sometimes people wonder when they pray what sort of a mood God is in. Is he angry with me? Is he too busy with someone else's problems to worry about mine? Although God is there to do us good, we might have a mental picture of him which makes us almost afraid to trouble him!

When we come to pray we need to remember what the Bible tells us about God:

1   **When you pray, say, 'Our Father'** (Matthew 6:9). God does not want you to pray as though he was some kind of great ogre sneering down from the window of heaven! He wants you to approach him as though he was a Father who loves you very much.

2   **'Come near to God and he will come near to you'** (James 4:8). Sometimes we think God has a real downer on us and we imagine that when he sees us entering our prayer space he evacuates the area as quickly as possible. Not at all! This verse promises that when we approach God he says, 'Oh great! Here comes Mark (Sarah or whoever)! I'll get a bit closer so I can hear what's on his mind!'

3   **'The Lord is merciful and loving, slow to become angry and full of constant love'** (Psalm 103:8). True, sometimes God *does* get angry with us when we keep on and on and on doing the same wrong things without ever attempting to put them right. But he is s-l-o-w to become angry. His anger is just a temporary (if unpleasant) blip. Once we put things right, he forgives and forgets *instantly* because basically his character is merciful, and full of constant love!!

prayer aid

1

Come clean
[telling God you're sorry]

Some things are very hard to say. Try saying 'the big burly bloke's back brake block broke'. OK. Now try saying it several times fast. OK. Now try saying it several times fast with a mouth full of Mars Bar. You see, some things ARE very hard to say.

Strangely, some very small words are also difficult to say. Take 'sorry' for example!

'Sorry' is difficult because for a small word it means so much!
It is really important to understand that when we sin (lie to our parents, nick sweets, spread gossip or whatever) that sin not only affects our friendship with the people concerned, but it also affects our relationship with God.

The Bible puts it this way:

'If I had ignored my sins, the Lord would not have listened to me.' (Psalm 66:18)

1   Sorry means, 'OK I agree with you; I was in the wrong.' To say sorry you need to admit that you are guilty – and that's not so easy. Say you lied to your parents about who you were out with last night. To say 'sorry' means that you admit that you lied and that lying is wrong.

2   Sorry means, 'I want to come clean and put this thing right.' When we do something wrong we feel guilty. Often our guilt spoils our relationship with the person whom we have wronged. If we lie to our parents, that lie makes it harder to relate to them. If we nick sweets from the local shop, that theft means that we avoid the shopkeeper as much as possible. If we spread rumours about a friend, that person probably doesn't stay a friend for very long! To say sorry is the first step to mending broken friendships.

3   Sorry means, 'I won't do it again.' What is the point of saying sorry for something you fully intend to repeat at the earliest opportunity?!

To say sorry to God is therefore vital if we want God to hear our prayers! When we say sorry to God we are really saying something like this:

**'OK I agree with you I was in the wrong.
I want to come clean and put this thing right.
I really never want to do this thing again.
Please forgive me.'**

When we say sorry like that, God has promised to forgive us *instantly* and *completely*. The friendship-blocking barrier of our sin is demolished and God can respond to our prayers.

What To Do Each Day

1 Chill out and focus on God.

2 Try to worship God each day using some of the songs, readings and ideas from the last two weeks.

3 When you have finished worshipping God, pray this prayer:

'Lord God, if I have said, thought or done anything that has offended you today I want to know about it. And if I haven't done everything that I should have done, I want to know about that too. Please show me now.'

4 Sit quietly for a few moments and allow the Holy Spirit to bring to mind any things that you need to confess. Make a note of them on a piece of scrap paper.

5 Use the 'Saying Sorry' prayers in *Prayer File 2* (p22) to say sorry for the things that you have done wrong.

6 Tell yourself: 'if I have confessed, God has promised to forgive.'

7 Write 'SORTED' in big letters on the scrap of paper – right across the list of things you've said sorry for. Now throw the paper in the bin!!

'Jesus said to them, "When you pray, say this... forgive us our sins".'

Luke 11:2,4

Sunday:
When you have worshipped and said sorry, sit and think about this verse: 'The Lord is merciful and loving, slow to become angry and full of constant love' (Psalm 103:8).

Monday:
When you have worshipped and said sorry, look at the picture of Jesus on his cross (p33). Think about the price of your forgiveness.

Tuesday:
When you have worshipped and said sorry, write a thank you letter to Jesus, thanking him for dying for your sins.

Wednesday:
When you have worshipped and said sorry, sit and think about this verse: 'God never bears a grudge, nor remains angry for ever' (Psalm 103:9, Living Bible).

Thursday:
When you have worshipped and said sorry, ask God to show you anyone whom you need to forgive. If anyone comes to mind write their name here and pray for the strength to do it: ....
....
....
....

Friday:
When you have worshipped and said sorry, sit and think about this verse: 'He has removed our sins as far away from us as the east is from the west' (Psalm 103:12, Living Bible). How far is that?!

Saturday:
When you have worshipped and said sorry, think back over the whole week and thank God for all that he has forgiven you for.

[YOU WRITE DATE]

DAYS OF THE WEEK

WEEK STARTING SUNDAY:

SUN
MON
TUES
WED
THUR
FRI
SAT

web site

I WORSHIPPED

I SAID SORRY

prayer log 3 web site

For instructions for what to do this week see page 17.

When you say sorry to God, try kneeling down as a sign of your regret at hurting him.

Don't forget to shade in the *Prayer web* each day that you worship and say sorry.

'God, if you kept a record of our sins, who could escape being condemned? But you forgive us.'

Psalm 130:3,4

Sunday:
When you have worshipped and said sorry, ask God for strength to do what is right in this new week.

Monday:
When you have worshipped and said sorry, think about the last eight days. Have you found yourself saying sorry for the same thing over and over again? Write that particular problem here and ask God to set you free from it: ....
....
....

Tuesday:
When you have worshipped and said sorry, once again, ask God's help with whatever you wrote down yesterday.

Wednesday:
When you have worshipped and said sorry, sit and think about this verse: 'Your sins are forgiven for the sake of Christ' (1 John 2:12).

Thursday:
When you have worshipped and said sorry, ask God to show you anyone whom you need to say sorry to. If anyone comes to mind, write their name here and pray for the opportunity to put things right:
....
....
....

Friday:
When you have worshipped and said sorry, sit and think about this verse: Jesus 'endured the suffering that should have been ours, the pain that we should have borne' (Isaiah 53:4). Look again at the picture on page 33 and thank Jesus for his love.

Saturday:
When you have worshipped and said sorry, look back over this week's and last week's **Prayer Logs** and underline the Bible verse on the theme of forgiveness that means the most to you.

prayer log

[YOU WRITE DATE]

WEEK STARTING SUNDAY:

DAYS OF THE WEEK

SUN
MON
TUES
WED
THUR
FRI
SAT

web site

I WORSHIPPED

I SAID SORRY

prayer log 4 web site

For instructions for what to do this week see page 17.

Try to complete the given tasks each day but if you don't manage it, *don't give up!* Just try to get back into routine on the next day.

Telling God you're sorry

Here is an outline 'sorry' prayer. Add in the things that you want to confess at the appropriate places.

Be specific; don't pray 'in-case-I-did-anything-wrong-I'm-sorry' sort of prayers.

Think of things you have THOUGHT, SAID or DONE wrong or anything that you know you SHOULD HAVE DONE which you didn't.

Dear Father,

I really blew it again today.

I ....

I've got no excuses and I won't try to wriggle out of taking responsibility for my actions. I agree with you that what I did was wrong.

Please forgive me and help me to cut this problem right out of my life.

I know that your Son Jesus died to take my punishment for these sins and that hurts me even more. Thank you, Jesus, for paying for my sin with your life.

Finally, Father, I want to thank you that you are so kind and generous that even as I confess this sin you have forgiven and forgotten completely. Thanks that you can forgive more times than I can sin! Cool!!

A 'sorry' prayer from the Bible.

Oh God, don't keep looking at my sins – erase them from your sight. Create in me a new, clean heart, O God, filled with clean thoughts and right desires. Don't toss me aside, banished for ever from your presence. Don't take your Holy Spirit from me. Restore to me again the joy of your salvation, and make me willing to obey you. (Psalm 51:9–12, Living Bible)

Body Language – What's yours saying?

I'm sure you've seen people at a football match 'worshipping' their team. They clap when the team comes onto the pitch, sing when their team needs encouragement, and jump up and down with their arms in the air when they score a goal! Why do they get so involved? Are they mad? No. Their behaviour is just a natural response to their feelings about their team. If they just sat still and quiet all through the game you might wonder whether they were genuine supporters at all!

The Bible is full of examples of people who were so excited or impressed by being near to God that their whole bodies expressed their feelings.

Here's some biblical 'worship body language':

Kneeling down – kneeling is a sign of respect for God's greatness, eg see Psalm 95:6; Ezra 9:5;

Bowing to the ground – this is a sign of great awe in God's presence, and can be a sign of sorrow for sin, eg see Exodus 4:31; Leviticus 9:23,24;

Lifting hands – this can be a sign of asking for help, almost as though we are reaching out to God to fill our outstretched hands, eg see Psalm 28:2; 143:6;

Clapping – this is a sign of gratitude, joy and happiness, eg Psalm 47:1;

Dancing – this is also a way of praising God for what he has done, eg Psalm 149:3; 150:4;

Slumped in an armchair – OK. This is not found anywhere in the Bible because it is a sign of being bored, fed up or switched off and therefore no way to approach God!!

The important thing is to know that it's OK to do these things because they are in your heart and not just because people in the Bible did them. If you are worshipping God and you feel like kneeling, then kneel; if you feel like dancing, then dance (might be wise to pull the curtains first!!).

Try it. Worship God with your body – it'll take you into another dimension!

Cool, God!

[telling God you're grateful]

Noddy got out of bed and said, 'Thank you, little bed for holding me up all night, so snug and comfortable between your fleecy sheets.'

He bent down and put on his little red shoes. 'Thank you, shoes, for keeping my feet warm and dry,' he said.

As Noddy placed his hat on his head, the merry tinkle of the little bell made his heart dance with joy and he cried out, 'Thank you, little bell, for accompanying all my movements with your sweet music.'

Walking across the room he drew back the curtains, letting in the bright morning sunshine. 'Thank you, sunshine, for shining so brightly and making the morning warm and cheerful,' he said.

He saw Big Ears out in the garden, and a flood of happiness almost overwhelmed him as he realised how good it was to have such a loyal, faithful friend. Noddy opened his window and shouted, 'Thank you, Big Ears, for being my good, loyal, faithful friend.'

And Big Ears said, 'Will you shut up and get down here. You've overslept and you're making me late.'

It's *good* to get into the habit of saying 'thanks' to God, but we will struggle to do so if we see God as a kind of heavenly Big Ears! God is *not* grumpy and he is *not* unmoved by hearing us say 'thank you'. In fact, the Bible gives the impression that it makes God really happy when we bother to say 'thanks', and disappointed when we take him for granted. So the first reason for giving thanks is because it makes God happy!

A second reason for saying 'thanks' is because it makes us focus on the good things in our lives – and that is a healthy thing for us to do. *Everyone* has hassles, but if we spend too much time thinking – or even praying – about them, it can make us negative and depressed. On the other hand, if we deliberately find things to thank for, the effect is to cheer us up.

A third reason for regularly saying 'thanks' to God is because it gets right up Satan's nose. He wants to make us believe that God is bad, that God doesn't love us, doesn't forgive us and doesn't hear our prayers. When Satan hears us say 'thanks' for what God *has* done, he knows he has failed to convince us!

Take time to say thanks for something every day. You'll please God, cheer yourself up and seriously dischuff Satan!!

What To Do Each Day   weeks 5+6

1   Go to your prayer space and chill out for a few minutes.

2   Continue to start your prayer time with worship using the CD, ideas from weeks 1 and 2 (p10–13) or other readings, prayers or songs that help you worship God.

3   Continue to use the exercises from the last two weeks to help you 'come clean' with God by saying sorry.

4   Each day you will be given some pointers to what to thank God for that day. You need to think of things that are real for you and write them in the space in that day's *Prayer Log*.

prayer *log*

Be thankful in all circumstances. This is what God wants from you...

1 Thessalonians 5:18

Sunday:
Thank God for three people at your church; write their names here:
....
....
....

Monday:
Thank God for three friends from school; write their names here:
....
....
....

Tuesday:
Thank God for any three items from the 'Thanks' collage (p34); write your choices here:...
....
....

Wednesday:
Thank God for three things about yourself; write them here:
....
....
....

Thursday:
Thank God for your favourite three possessions; list them here:
....
....
....

Friday:
Use some of the prayers in *Prayer File 3* on page 30 and make them your own.

Saturday:
Thank God for three things that you feel good about from this past week; write them here:...
....
....

Use the song 'Hosanna' (track 1 on the CD) to express your gratitude to God.

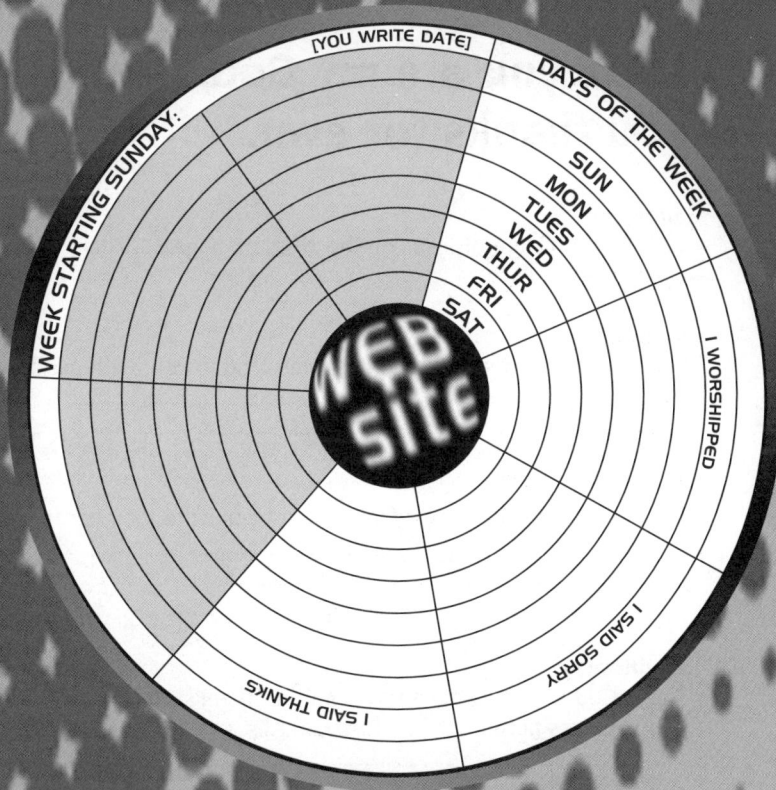

The prayer web wheel contains:
- WEEK STARTING SUNDAY:
- [YOU WRITE DATE]
- DAYS OF THE WEEK
- SUN
- MON
- TUES
- WED
- THUR
- FRI
- SAT
- WEB site
- I WORSHIPPED
- I SAID SORRY
- I SAID THANKS

For instructions for what to do this week see page 25.

When you say your prayers of thanks, try standing up and punching the air as you say the word 'Thanks!'

Don't forget to shade in the Prayer Web to show which days you worship, say sorry and say thanks.

Make a list here of all the things and people that you've thanked God for this week: ....
....
....
....

Refer back to this 'Personal Praise List' in coming weeks.

Lord, you are my God, I will give you thanks for ever.

Psalm 30:12

Sunday:
Turn to the picture of Jesus on the cross on page 33. Thank him for dying in your place.

Monday:
Thank God for a teacher who has been kind to you; write his/her name here: ....
....

Tuesday:
Thank God for your closest family members; write their names here:
....
....
....

Wednesday:
Thank God for any three items from the 'Thanks' collage (p34); write your choices here: ....
....
....

Thursday:
Thank God for any particular skills or gifts that he has given you; write them here: ....
....
....

Friday:
Thank God for your three favourite things from the world of nature; write them here:..
....
....

Saturday:
Thank God for anyone who has encouraged you this week; write their name(s) here: ....
....
....

prayer log

[YOU WRITE DATE]

DAYS OF THE WEEK

WEEK STARTING SUNDAY:

SUN
MON
TUES
WED
THUR
FRI
SAT

WEB site

I WORSHIPPED

I SAID SORRY

I SAID THANKS

prayer log 6 web site

If you feel you have nothing to say thanks for, turn to page 45!

Remember to shade in the Prayer Web each day that you worship, say sorry and say thanks.

Make a list here of all the things you've thanked God for this week:

....
....
....
....
....
....

Refer back to this 'Personal Praise List' in coming weeks.

Telling God
you're grateful

THANKS FOR GOOD MATES

Father God, thanks for my mates. They help me when I'm stuck, cheer me up when I'm down and entertain me when I'm bored. They're OK; thanks. And thanks especially for my Christian friends who help me keep my life aimed at you.

THANKS FOR PARENTS

Father God, thanks for my parent(s). I know they get a lot wrong but they have also got a lot right! Thanks that they care about me and have looked after me all these years (changing my nappies must have been gross). Thanks that they have loved me – even when I haven't been able to thank them!

THANKS FOR WEATHER

Father God, thanks for weather! It makes life interesting especially when it's kind of extreme. Thanks for snow, thunder, gales and burning sunshine; and thanks that it doesn't all come at once!

THANKS FOR JESUS

Father God, thanks for sending your son Jesus into the world to die for my sins. You must have hated to see him suffer; thanks for going through with it for me. Thanks to you, Jesus, for putting up with being laughed at, spat at and crucified so that I could be let off my sins. Your courage and love are just excellent; thanks so much.

THANKS FOR FORGIVENESS

Father God, I find it really hard to keep forgiving people who hurt me or let me down, but you just keep on and on offering to forgive me every time I foul up. Thanks. I hate feeling guilty, so thanks again that every time I'm really sorry, you're really forgiving!

THANKS FOR FOOD

Father God, I love eating! THANKS that I live in a part of the world where I can have enough. Thanks for pizza, peanut butter and satsumas*. Thanks for Big Macs, French Fries and those gorgeous apple pies that come so hot they burn the skin off your tongue if you're not careful! Thanks.
*(Substitute your fave nosh for those suggested!)

Come clean

[saying sorry to God] REVISITED

How not to forfeit your forgiveness

There was once a man called Hard-Hearted Harold who owed King Kindheart III squillions of pounds. Harold couldn't repay his huge debt to King Kindheart so the king ordered that he should be sold as a slave, together with his wife and children in order to raise the money that he owed!! Even King Kindheart had to carry out the law!

Harold fell on his knees and begged to be forgiven and the kind, tender-hearted king felt sorry for him, let him off the millions that he owed and let him go free, clutching a royally signed Certificate of Forgiveness. What a mega-merciful monarch was King Kindheart III!

Harold wandered outside and spied a friend (Begging-Bowl Barry) who owed him three pounds. He jumped on him, grabbed him around the throat and screamed, 'Pay me back my three pounds.' Barry was a very poor man and didn't have three pounds but he was also fair. He said, 'I can't pay you today but if you're patient I'll go without my dinner every day and pay you back as soon as I possibly can.' Harold would have none of it. Despite the fact that he had just been forgiven his multi-million pound debt by King Kindheart III he insisted that Barry be sent to prison until he could pay back the measly three quid that he owed.

Well, when King Kindheart got to hear of Hard-Hearted Harold's harsh treatment of Begging-Bowl Barry, he was furious and ordered Harold to come back before him. Harold trembled like a jelly on a skateboard as he stood before the king. Kindheart III tore up Harold's Certificate of Forgiveness saying, 'If you refuse to forgive other people after all that I've forgiven you, then I withdraw my forgiveness from you. You must go to jail and be punished until you pay back all that you owe. See how you like it!'

And Jesus concluded, 'That is how my Father in heaven will treat every one of you unless you forgive your brother from your heart.'

[*You can read this story in Matthew 18:21–35.*]

God's forgiveness is free! You say 'sorry' and he WILL forgive you because he has a kind heart. But we must then make sure we are equally forgiving of other people or we forfeit our own forgiveness. It's no good asking God to forgive us if we are holding a grudge against other people.

Is there anyone on this list you need to forgive in order to receive God's forgiveness?

- ○ **Parents**
- ○ **Teachers**
- ○ **Brother/sister**
- ○ **Friend**
- ○ **Ex-friend!**
- ○ **An 'enemy'**

Go and put things right as soon as possible.

AH PING

As a young woman, Jackie Pullinger felt that God was telling her to go to Hong Kong. With only just enough money for her boat ticket (one way!) she set out for Hong Kong, not knowing what awaited her. When she arrived she soon found herself sharing Jesus with violent members of the Triad gangs that lived in a very rough area called the 'walled city'. A young man called Ah Ping was the first Triad gangster to join the Christians. This is Jackie Pullinger's account of what happened to him on the way home from a Christian meeting not long after becoming a Christian:

'As if from nowhere seven men jumped out of a black alley and attacked him. They were Chiu Chow gangsters, big for Chinese, and wild fighters. There was no reason for their attack, but that did not stop it coming. Later Ah Ping told me, "As they came at me I had two thoughts. First of all, 'Huh, it's all Miss Poon's fault', and then, 'you're supposed to pray".' So he prayed as the wooden bats beat him unconscious into the ground.

' "Didn't do you much good praying, did it?" scoffed one of his friends when he heard the story.

' "Yes it did," retorted Ah Ping. "I'll tell you why. As soon as I began to pray, my father came down the street and when the Chiu Chows saw him, they ran away. Otherwise I would have been killed."

'As it was, he was left on the ground with a gash in his back and a hole in his throat. His father summoned help from his gang brothers. They found him and took him to a doctor who gave it as his professional opinion that his injuries were so bad that he would not be able to walk or speak for at least two weeks.

'Forbidding his gang brothers to take revenge on his behalf, Ah Ping, speaking through his injured throat, asked for one or two friends who were believers to pray with him.

'All night they prayed for the gang who attacked him and also laid their hands on Ah Ping to pray for his healing.

'The next morning he was completely healed, and he could talk clearly. In fact he spoke in church just two days later!

Extract from *Chasing the Dragon* by Jackie Pullinger
Copyright © 1980 by Jackie Pullinger and Andrew Quicke
Reproduced by permission of Hodder and Stoughton Limited

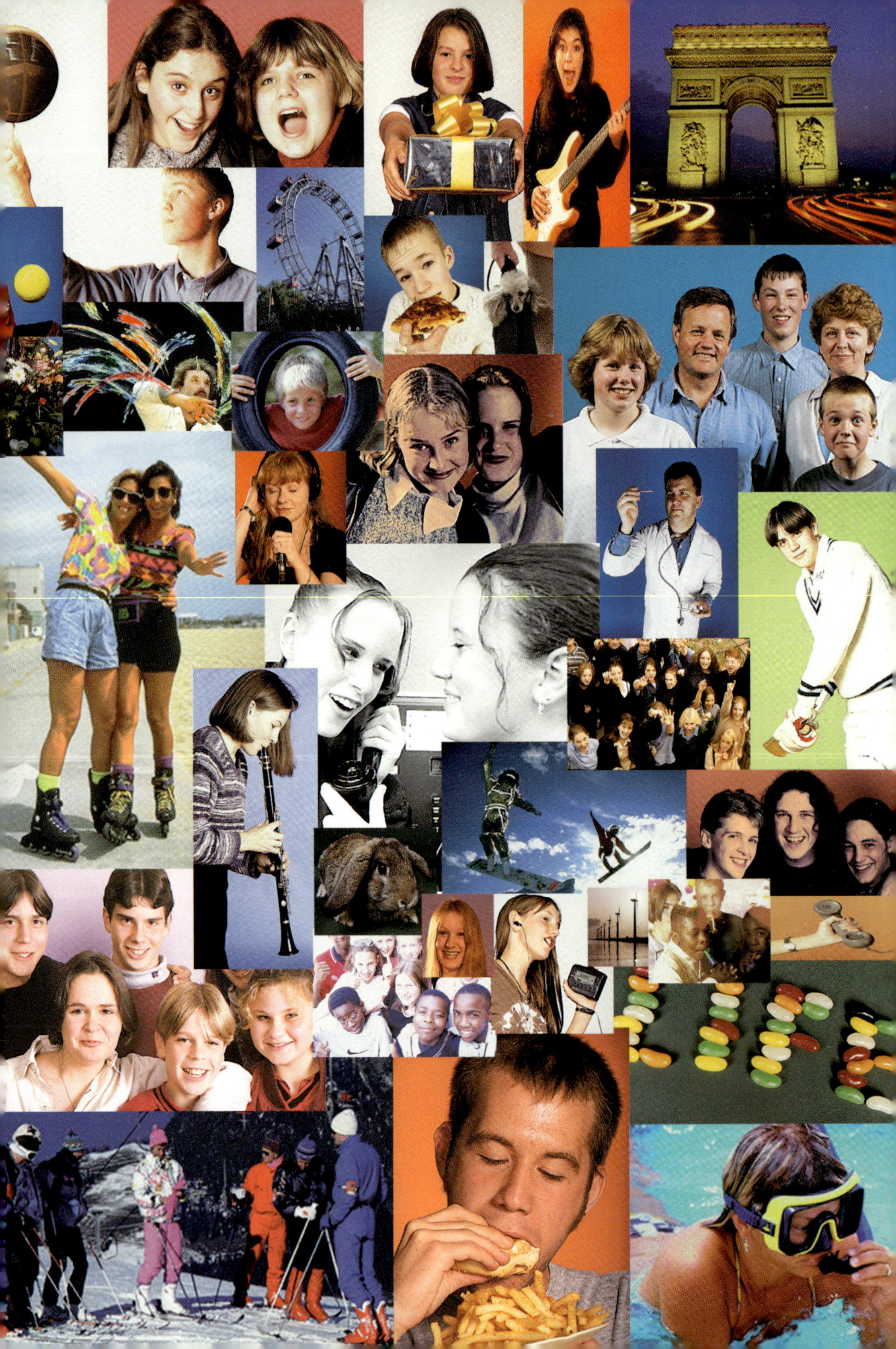

O Lord, our Lord,
your GREATNESS
is seen in all the world
Psalm 8:9

© Zefa

The 10/40 Window

Believe it
– or not ?

It's a fact that many people 'say their prayers' without any great belief that God can actually make much difference to the things that they are praying about!!

Ask yourself, when you pray do you *really* believe that God is going to get on the job and answer you? This conviction that God is going to answer (in whatever way he wants and whenever he chooses) **is vital to powerful praying.**

The Bible has lots of verses which emphasise how important it is to pray with faith. Praying *with faith* simply means that when you ask God for something you believe that he is *concerned* enough and *powerful* enough to answer you.

Say you were praying for a friend who had become ill. Ask yourself before you pray, 'Do I really

believe that God is concerned about this person?' and 'Do I really believe that God is powerful enough to help her?' To pray with faith would require you to answer 'yes' to both questions.

Here are some Bible verses to inspire faith-filled praying:

'Call to me and I will answer you' (Jeremiah 33:3).

'No-one can please God without faith, for whoever comes to God must have faith that God exists and rewards those who seek him' (Hebrews 11:6).

'We have courage in God's presence, because we are sure that he hears us if we ask him for anything that is according to his will ... We know also that he gives us what we ask from him' (1 John 5:14,15).

prayer aid 2

Dear God – help!

[asking God for what you need]

Dear Lord,
Hi! Jamie here. Listen I haven't got long but you've got to help me cos I'm in a real fix. I've got a science test this morning and I haven't done any revision. If I don't get at least half marks Mum is going to ground me, my teacher's going to do my head in and Clarissa (you know, Lord, the one I fancy) is going to think I'm a real no-hoper. Please fix it Lord. And seeing as how I've mentioned Clarissa, any chance of a bit of help in that direction too? Cheers. Oh, er... in Jesus' name. Amen.

Far-fetched or all too near the truth? Sometimes if we could only stop and listen to our prayers they might not sound too different from Jamie's! So how do we pray for ourselves? Here is some advice from Jesus himself!

1 **Be yourself.** You don't have to use special words or a different voice to speak to God. Nor do you have to say long prayers in case God hasn't tuned in at the beginning! Read Matthew 6:7.

2 **Ask for what God wants.** Jesus said that the secret of prayer is to ask for God's 'will to be done on earth as it is in heaven' (Matthew 6:10). This can be tricky but try to think 'What does God want for my life?' not 'What do I want for my life?' – there can be a difference! (For more help on understanding what God wants for your life see *Asking God for what you need – revisited* on page 55.)

3 **Ask for what you need.** There is a difference between what we *want* to make life more pleasant and what we *need* to make life possible. Jesus said to pray for the 'food we need' (Matthew 6:11) not the 'feast you want'! You may want a pair of Kickers but you don't actually *need* them, so maybe you shouldn't be asking for them.

*intro*ducing

4 **Ask for protection.** Every day we are surrounded by the threat of evil and the temptation to do wrong. Jesus said that we should ask God our Father not to 'bring us to hard testing but keep us safe from the Evil One' (Matthew 6:13).

5 **Ask for forgiveness for your mistakes.** Jesus said that we should ask God to 'forgive us the wrongs that we have done' (Matthew 6:12). Remind yourself of what you have already learned about this aspect of prayer by revisiting pages 16, 17 and 22.

6 **Make sure you have forgiven everyone.** Yesterday's unresolved row with Mum may not appear to have anything to do with praying for what you need but according to Jesus it has. If we will not forgive other people God will not forgive us (Matthew 6:12,14) and our prayer life will get blocked. (See *Why doesn't God answer me?* on page 46 and *Come clean – revisited* on page 31).

What To Do Each Day   weeks 7+8

1 Go to your prayer space and chill out for a few minutes.

2 Continue to start your prayer time with worship, using the CD, ideas from weeks 1 and 2 (p10–13) or your own worship songs and prayers.

3 Continue to make space to say 'sorry' to God. Use the ideas from weeks 3 and 4 (p17–22).

4 Continue to find things each day to thank God for. Refer to your *Personal Praise* on pages 27 and 29.

5 Each day's *Prayer Log* for weeks 7 and 8 leaves you plenty of space to write down the things that you want to pray for yourself each day. There may be a big thing on your mind which you pray for every day or each day may be different; either way write down your personal prayer list each day.

6 In the box in the bottom right hand corner of page 41 write down any answers to your prayers as the week goes on.

'I pray to you, O God, because you answer me; so turn to me and listen to my words.'

Psalm 17:6

Sunday:
My personal prayer requests today are...

....

....

Monday:
My personal prayer requests today are...

....

....

Tuesday:
My personal prayer requests today are...

....

....

Wednesday:
My personal prayer requests today are...

....

....

Thursday:
My personal prayer requests today are...

....

....

Friday:
My personal prayer requests today are...

....

....

Saturday:
My personal prayer requests today are...

....

....

prayer *log*

[YOU WRITE DATE]

DAYS OF THE WEEK

WEEK STARTING SUNDAY:

SUN
MON
TUES
WED
THUR
FRI
SAT

WEB site

I WORSHIPPED

I PRAYED FOR MYSELF

I SAID SORRY

I SAID THANKS

prayer log 7 web site

For instructions for what to do this week see page 39.

Don't forget to shade in the *Prayer Web* to show which days you worship, say sorry, say thanks and pray for yourself.

Write any answers to prayer here: ....

....

....

....

....

....

....

....

....

Don't worry about anything, but in all your prayers ask God for what you need.

Philippians 4:6

Sunday:
Use the song 'Touch my life' from the CD (track 6) as your prayer for yourself today and throughout this week (words are on page 44).

Monday:
My personal prayer requests today are...

....

....

Tuesday:
My personal prayer requests today are...

....

....

Wednesday:
My personal prayer requests today are...

....

....

Thursday:
My personal prayer requests today are...

....

....

Friday:
My personal prayer requests today are...

....

....

Saturday:
My personal prayer requests today are...

....

....

prayer*log*

The circular prayer web diagram contains the following labels:

[YOU WRITE DATE]

DAYS OF THE WEEK

WEEK STARTING SUNDAY:

SUN
MON
TUES
WED
THUR
FRI
SAT

WEB site

I WORSHIPPED

I SAID SORRY

I SAID THANKS

I PRAYED FOR MYSELF

prayer log 8 web site

If you don't manage to pray every day, don't give up! Every day is a new beginning. Shade in the *Prayer Web* to keep track of your prayer life.

Write any answers to prayer here: ....
....
....
....
....
....
....
....
....
....

Asking God
for what you need

When I'm sick

Lord, I'm feeling really rough right now. Jesus, I know that you healed loads of people of all kinds of illnesses when you were on earth and I believe that you can still do the same today. Please help me get better. Thanks. Amen.
[For a great story of God answering a healing prayer see Ah Ping's story on page 32.]

When I'm scared

Father, you are Almighty but I am all talk.
Jesus, you are a warrior but I am a worrier.
Spirit, you are powerful but I feel puny.

Father, encircle me today with your almighty love.
Jesus, fight on my behalf in the battles of tomorrow.
Spirit, empower me to stand strong and true to the end of the day.

Touch my life

Touch my life, O Lord my God,
Holy fire come.
Touch my lips that I might speak
Of the wonders of your Son.

Chorus: Your Spirit's anointing I desire,
The power of God;
To demonstrate justice, Lord, I need
The power of God;
To tell of your healing and release,
The power of God.

Touch my heart, O Lord my God,
Cleanse me with your blood.
Fill me with your Spirit, Lord,
Flow through me like a flood.

Derek Bond © Daybreak Music Ltd

When I'm alone

Jesus, tonight I feel so alone. No-one seems to understand me and even my best friends have deserted me. Thanks that you never leave me and that you always love me – even when I blow it. Comfort me tonight and as tomorrow unfolds help me to find someone who will accept me as I am and treat me as a friend. Amen.

Cool, God!

OK. You've had a bad day.

You had an 'oversleeping-breakfastmissing-schoolbuslate' start, followed by a 'testfailing-teachermoaning-dinnermoneylosing' day at Freda's Academic and Intellectual Learning School (FAIL school for short!). You then suffer a 'suddendownpour-coatforgetting-doorkeylosing' journey home and enjoy a 'TVbusted-homeworkinfested-littlesisterafflicted' evening.

Now you are all set up to give THANKS to God; right? Wrong!

When we have had a bad day, it is that much harder just to slip into 'thanks mode'. But it is perhaps *especially* when we have had a bad day that we need to find some reasons for thanking God.

Back on page 25 we saw that finding things to thank God for can actually have the effect of cheering us up – of reminding us that not absolutely *everything* is bad. Here are some reasons that the Bible says we should thank God, reasons that are true on good days *and* bad days.

Look up
Because God is always good and his love never runs out (Psalm 107:1). How does God feel about you on a bad day, even on a day when you have done, said or thought some wrong things? He loves you. He loved you yesterday and today and he will love you tomorrow. He is in love with you (which is why it hurts him so much when you don't love him back!). The fact that his love is eternal is a reason to say 'thanks'.

Look forward
Because, ultimately, God will put right all of the unfair things in the world (see Psalm 7:17). The world is full of unkind, unfair and unjust actions. Innocent people get hurt; maybe you are one of them! The Bible promises that God will work justice when Jesus returns so that evil is punished and good is rewarded. The promise of wrongs being righted is a reason to say 'thanks'.

Look back
Because, even if today has been horrific, we can remember good things that God has done in the past (see Psalm 75:1). Look back and thank God for what he HAS done by referring to your praise points on pages 26–29. Doing that will also give you confidence that God can do it again!

Why doesn't God answer me?

prayer aid 3

Sometimes we think that God has been mean or uncaring when he doesn't give us what we asked for. The problem of 'unanswered prayer' is not an easy one, but the Bible does give us some answers as to why God, at times, remains silent or does the opposite of what we'd hoped for. Here are some of the reasons:

1 **'You do not have what you want because you do not ask God for it!' (James 4:2).**
OK, it's obvious but let's state it anyway. If you stop asking you'll stop getting! God will not answer unspoken prayers.

2 **'When you pray, you must believe and not doubt at all.' (James1:6.)**
Do you really believe that God can do what you are asking of him (see *Prayer Aid 2* on page 37)? God will not answer faith-less prayers.

3 **'When you ask you do not receive it, because your motives are bad; you ask for things to use for your own pleasures' (James 4:3).**
Prayer is a way of understanding and asking for what God wants done, not for twisting his arm to give us our own way! God will not answer selfish prayers.

4 **'The prayer of a good person has a powerful effect.' (James 5:16).**
The Bible says: 'If I had ignored my sins, the Lord would not have listened to me' (Psalm 66:18). We need to put things right with God – and with others – before we pray (see pages 16,31). God will not ignore unconfessed sin to answer our prayers.

5 **'See how patient a farmer is as he waits for his land to produce crops ... You also must be patient' (James 5:7,8).**
A farmer may not understand why it takes a long time for his corn to grow; he just knows that he has to be patient whilst it does so. We may not understand why God takes a long time to answer some of our prayers but we must be patient and trust him to do the right thing at the right time. (He is God after all!!)

BROTHER ANDREW

Have you seen the exciting television pictures from the late 1980s of the Berlin Wall coming down? The wall was a symbol of the great divide between the Communist countries of Eastern Europe and the democratic countries of Western Europe. During the years of Communist rule many Christians in eastern Europe had a really tough time. Some were arrested, tortured and even executed for their faith; most were watched by the dreaded secret police.

Brother Andrew, a Dutch missionary, made it his business to smuggle much-needed Bibles into eastern Europe to encourage the Christians. This was a very dangerous thing to do since the Bible was a banned book. On one of his first trips into Hungary he had managed to cross the border with the Bibles hidden in the boot of his car. By the side of the river Danube he stopped to eat and as he did so heard the roar of a speedboat racing towards him at top speed. The boat carried armed soldiers who leapt ashore as the boat drew to the river's edge.

As they approached his car Brother Andrew quietly prayed, 'Lord, help me refuse to yield to fear.'

One soldier pointed his machine gun at Brother Andrew as the other searched the car, including the boot! As he did so, Brother Andrew's simple meal which he had been cooking on a small camping stove was hot enough to eat. With great courage, right beneath the glare of the Communist soldiers he bowed his head, folded his hands and said long and hearty thanks to God for the food which he was about to eat!

This, in his own words, is what happened next.

'An amazing thing happened. While I prayed there was no sound from the soldier inspecting my car. Just as soon as I had finished, the door slammed and I heard the sound of boots coming rapidly towards me. I picked up my fork and took a bite of peas. For a moment both soldiers stood over me. Then abruptly they whirled. Without looking behind them, they ran down to their boat, jumped in, and roared off in a spray of white!'

The Bibles were safely delivered to Budapest and Brother Andrew had proved the power of prayer. He had asked for freedom from fear and God had enabled him to act in a very courageous way despite being in danger. He had asked for the Bibles to be kept safe and God somehow kept them safe from discovery by the soldiers!

Extract from *God's Smuggler* by Brother Andrew
Copyright © 1967 by Brother Andrew and John and Elizabeth Sherrill
Reproduced by permission of Hodder and Stoughton Limited.

people who prayed

Standing
in the gap
[asking God for what others need]

intro*ducing*

One of the great things about prayer is that we can help all sorts of people all over the world without ever leaving our prayer space! Imagine making a difference to that friend at school who was upset today, the person at church who has to go into hospital tomorrow, the church's missionary in Albania – not to mention the Prime Minister of England, the President of the USA and the poor people of Haiti! We really can 'touch the world through prayer'!

There are many examples of Bible characters praying for others. Here are some of the people who get prayed for:

- Kings and all people in authority, eg politicians, teachers (1 Timothy 2:2)

- People who are sick (James 5:15)

- Christian ministers and missionaries (Ephesians 6:19)

- Christians in other countries (Romans 1:8)

- Christian friends (John 17:9–15)

- People in trouble or danger (Acts 12:5)

- Our enemies! (Matthew 5:44)

- People who are not yet Christians (but who might be one day) (John 17:20)

- Family members (Mark 5:22,23)

For each of the above categories, make a 'Prayer hit list' of people to pray for by filling the empty boxes with names of people that you know need your prayers. Try to put a name in each of the four boxes in each category.

	❶	❷	❸	❹
kings and people in authority				
people who are sick				
ministers and missionaries				
Christians in other countries				
Christian friends				
people in trouble or danger				
our enemies!				
not yet Christians				
family members				

What To Do Each Day

Before Friday, turn to *Standing in the gap – revisited* (p68) and read about praying for the world's most needy countries.

What to do each day

1 Go to your prayer space and chill out for a few minutes.

2 Continue to start your prayer time with worship.

3 Continue to make space to say 'sorry' to God.

4 Continue to thank God each day.

5 Continue to pray for your own needs.

6 Take time each day to pray for one or more of the people on your 'Prayer hit list' on this page. Feel free to add new names in or take people off when your prayers are answered – it's your list! When you pray:

● Pause to think exactly who you are praying for.
● Pause to think exactly what you are asking God to do for them.
● Pray a short, to-the-point prayer.
● Repeat the process for the next person.

Reminder: Don't forget the importance of praying with faith. God really can make a difference!! (Turn to the *Believe it – or not?* feature on page 37.)

If you believe, you will receive whatever you ask for in prayer.

Matthew 21:22

Sunday:
Choose four people from your 'People in Authority' and 'People who are Sick' hit lists (two from each list). Write their names here and pray for them:
....

Monday:
Choose four people from your 'Ministers and Missionaries' and 'Christians in other countries' hit lists. Write their names here and pray for them:
....

Tuesday:
Choose four people from your 'Christian Friends' and 'People in Trouble' hit lists. Write their names here and pray for them:
....

Wednesday:
Choose four people from your 'Enemies' and 'Not-Yet-Christians' hit lists. Write their names here and pray for them:
....

Thursday:
Choose four people from your 'Family' hit list. Write their names here and pray for them: ....

Friday:
Turn to *Standing in the gap – revisited* (p68). Choose two countries from your list, write them here and pray for them:
....

Saturday:
Look back through the people and countries that you have prayed for this week. Choose just one person or situation that is mega-needy. Use CD track 7 'This is your hour – come with power' as a prayer to ask God's power to touch the person or situation that you have identified.

prayer log

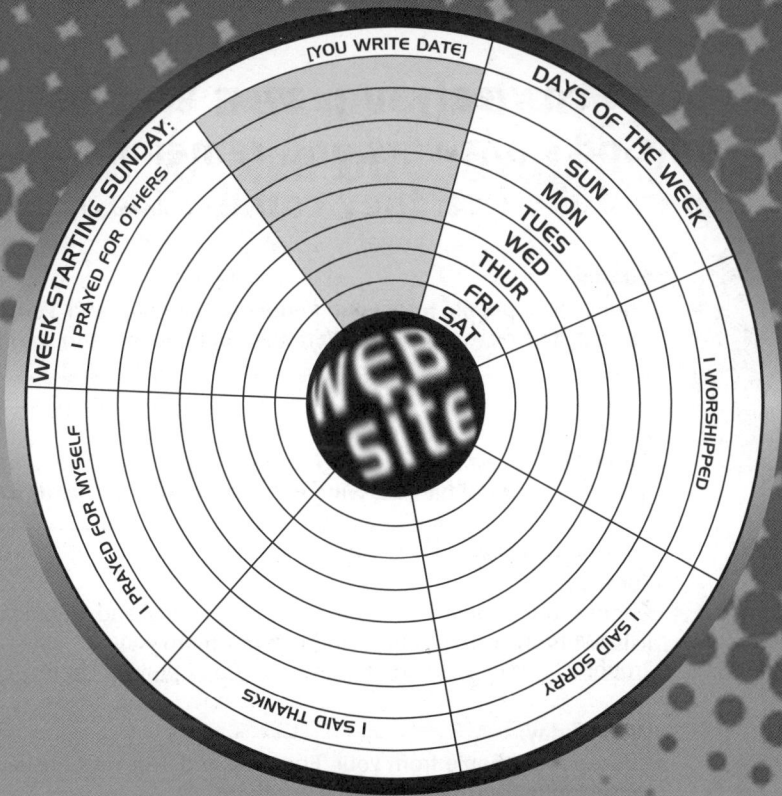

The circular prayer web diagram contains the following labels:

[YOU WRITE DATE]

DAYS OF THE WEEK

SUN
MON
TUES
WED
THUR
FRI
SAT

WEEK STARTING SUNDAY:

I PRAYED FOR OTHERS

I PRAYED FOR MYSELF

I SAID THANKS

I SAID SORRY

I WORSHIPPED

WEB site

prayer log 9 web site

For instructions for what to do this week see page 49.

Don't forget to shade in the *Prayer Web* to show which days you worship, say sorry, say thanks, pray for yourself and pray for others.

Write any answers to prayer here: ....
....
....
....
....
....
....
....
....
....

'Don't be weary in prayer; keep at it; watch for God's answers and remember to be thankful when they come' Colossians 4:2 (Living Bible).

Sunday:
Choose four people from your 'People in Authority' and 'Family members' hit lists (two from each list). Write their names here and pray for them:
....
....

Monday:
Choose four people from your 'People who are sick' and 'Enemies' hit lists. Write their names here and pray for them: ....
....

Tuesday:
Choose four people from your 'Ministers & Missionaries' and 'People in Trouble' hit lists. Write their names here and pray for them:
....
....

Wednesday:
Choose four people from your 'Christians in other churches' and 'Christian friends' hit lists. Write their names here and pray for them:
....
....

Thursday:
Choose two people from your 'Not-Yet-Christians' hit list. Write their name here and pray for them: ....
....

Friday:
Turn to *Standing in the gap – revisited* on page 68. Choose two countries from your list, write them here and pray for them: ....
....

Saturday:
Look back through the list of people and countries that you have prayed for this week. Choose just one person who is mega-needy and pray for them. Play the song 'O Lord Hear My Prayer' from the CD – track 8 – as you pray.

prayerlog

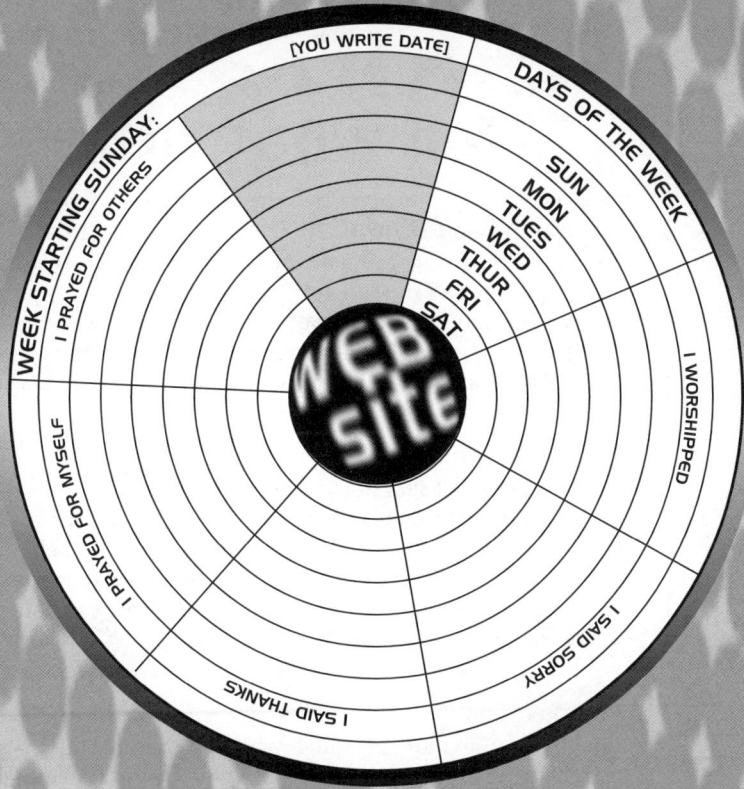

The *Prayer Web* circle:

[YOU WRITE DATE]

WEEK STARTING SUNDAY:

DAYS OF THE WEEK

SUN
MON
TUES
WED
THUR
FRI
SAT

WEB site

I PRAYED FOR OTHERS

I PRAYED FOR MYSELF

I SAID THANKS

I SAID SORRY

I WORSHIPPED

For instructions for what to do this week see page 49.

If you don't manage to pray every day, don't give up! Every day can be a new beginning. Shade in the *Prayer Web* to keep track of your prayer progress.

Write any answers to prayer here: ....
....
....
....
....
....
....
....
....

Asking God
for what others need

prayer file 5

For not-yet-Christian friends

Lord Jesus, I want to pray for my mate ....
(S)he's not a Christian yet. It's not that (s)he has rejected you; it's more like (s)he's just never given you a second thought! Could you get on the case and generate a bit of interest in her/him? And if (s)he starts asking me tough questions, give me the right answers! Ta!

For youth leaders

Lord, thanks for my youth group leaders. I know we take them for granted and sometimes give them grief, but Lord, tonight, I want to say 'thanks' for the time they give to help us. This week could you fix it for them to have at least one real encouragement in the work that they do. Give them energy, patience, skill and a better taste in music! Thanks God.

For enemies

Father God, I find it really tough when people take the mickey out of me. I hate being made to look small and I hate being laughed at. But Lord, you tell me that I must forgive my enemies and pray for them, so tonight I ask that you would bless .... even though they have made my life miserable today. Yeah, bless them Lord! They are probably the way they are because they are in a mess inside so help them get straightened out too. Thanks Lord.

For ministers and missionaries

For all who work to let others know about Jesus,
I pray your peace, power and protection from evil.
For all who have made sacrifices to work full-time for you,
I pray your peace, power and protection from evil.
For all who face hostility and rejection for sharing Jesus,
I pray your peace, power and protection from evil.
For all who are exhausted reaching the lost or serving your church,
I pray your peace, power and protection from evil.
For the ministers of my church ....(names)
I pray your peace, power and protection from evil.
For the missionaries that I know ....(names)
I pray your peace, power and protection from evil.
Amen.

Dear God – help! [asking God for what you need]

REVISITED

Back on page 38 we discovered that 'praying for ourselves' isn't quite as selfish as it sounds! Rather than just telling God what WE want, Jesus told us to pray for God's will to be done in our lives. Sounds easy enough but how do we know what God wants for us? Here are four questions to help you discover God's will:

1. *What does it say in the Bible?* The Bible teaches us what God is like and how he wants us to behave. For example. Jesus taught us not to take revenge on someone who wrongs us (Matthew 5:39) and so it would be wrong to pray for the opportunity to get even with your mum because in a fit of unreasonable anger she grounded you without listening to your side of the story!

2. *What do older Christians advise?* God frequently speaks through the mouths of other people. Older Christians may be God's resource bank for you to tap into so if you are stuck on how to pray for a particular issue, why not check it out with them. You may feel that God wants you to leave school to go as a missionary to the Bahamas, but it might be worth getting a second opinion on that!

3. *What does your conscience say?* Our feelings of guilt are often God's 'voice' telling us we've lost the plot and we are out of line. As you ask God for that new computer system you may feel a twinge of guilt about all the starving people in the world who have no potatoes, never mind silicon chips. Listen to your conscience and you may want to change what you pray for!

4. *What does the Holy Spirit have to say?* Sometimes when we pray, if we are quiet and listen to our thoughts the Holy Spirit might give us an idea or a mental picture of how God wants us to pray (see Time out – letting God speak on pages 56 and 57).

It is important to pray for what God wants but if you are still not sure what that is then just pour out whatever is on your mind anyway. God loves you enough to let you ask for anything but loves you too much to give you what is bad for you! So if you are not sure about God's will, pray the way that Jesus prayed before he was arrested, eg Lord, if it is possible this is what I would really like, 'not my will, however, but your will be done' (Luke 22:42).

Time out

[Letting God speak]

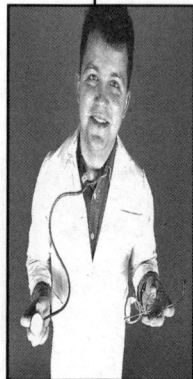

You are feeling unwell so you go to the doctor (just imagine). You enter his surgery and before he can even say 'inflamed epiglottis' you begin to explain your symptoms.

'My throat's really sore, my nose is bunged up and all night long I have this really nasty cough. I've got a headache some of the time and I reckon my temperature is quite high too. I think it's pretty obvious that I've got a heavy cold, possibly even flu so you ought to tell me to go home, take two paracetamol every four hours and stay in bed until I feel stronger. Thanks very much. I'm off now. Bye!'

The doctor is still trying to say 'hello' as you rush out of the door to catch the bus home!

Ridiculous? Well maybe, but it is all too similar to the way that a lot of us pray. We rush into God's presence, list everything that we can think of that's wrong with us, tell him what he should do about it and then rush off!

Have you ever considered that sometimes God may want to speak to *you* about something? So far we have been learning how to speak to God but in this final 'Introducing' section we pose the tricky question, 'How do we let God speak to us?' Here is a plan of action that we are going to try to put into practice in this coming week:

To let God speak...

1 **You need to *forget*.**
   Try to empty your mind of your thoughts and concerns and fill it with thoughts of God. It may help to repeat a simple prayer over and over again until you feel God is fairly central in your mind (see **Prayer File 6** on page 60).

2 **You need to *focus*.**
   God will often 'speak' to us as we *focus* our attention on something else. It might be:
   ● a Bible story or just one verse
   ● a picture
   ● a song
   ● an object

introducing

So once you have *forgotten* other concerns, begin to *focus* on the verse, picture, song or object that we will give you each day for the next week.

You really need to *focus* on the *focus*! So if the *focus* is a Bible story, read it through slowly lots of times and try to use your imagination. Think what it would have been like to be there; try to imagine the sights, sounds and smells of the scene. On the other hand if the *focus* is a picture, look at it for a good long time trying to notice every detail.

3 **You need to *fink* (er... THink, that is)!**
   As we give our attention to the *focus*, God might 'speak' to us by dropping ideas, words or pictures into our minds. For example:

   ● ideas might come into our heads about God or ourselves
   ● Bible verses or stories might come to mind
   ● we might feel unexpectedly happy... or sad
   ● we might begin to feel guilty about something
   ● we might sense that we should do something
     (eg ring a friend, apologise to a teacher)
   ● we might get a 'mental picture' of an image or scene.

Any of these thoughts and feelings COULD be God communicating his thoughts into our minds.

4 **You need to *follow*-through.**
   If God does 'speak' to you in any of these ways, it's important to *follow*-through by considering what you have 'heard' and acting on it.

   Write the ideas that God has placed in your mind in the spaces on the *Prayer Log* pages.

   Ask God to show you what they mean and keep thinking about them during the day.

   If you are really sure that God has put a thought into your mind and you cannot understand why, ask a youth leader or older Christian to explain it to you.

What To Do Each Day

1 **Go to your prayer space and chill out for a few minutes**

2 **Continue to incorporate worship, saying sorry, saying thanks, asking for what you need and asking for others in your prayer times. Don't worry if you spend longer on some bits than others.**

3 **Follow the F-plan *(forget, focus, fink, follow-through)* using the suggested focus for that day.**

Speak Lord, your servant is listening!

1 Samuel 3:9

Sunday:
Forget and *focus* on the picture on page 35. *Fink* and write any *follow*-through ideas here: ....
....

Monday:
Forget and *focus* on the picture on page 33 while listening to track 9 'Green Hill' from the CD. *Fink* and write any *follow*-through ideas here: ....
....

Tuesday:
Forget and *focus* on these words of Jesus: 'You are my friends if you do what I command you' (John 15:14). *Fink* and write any *follow*-through ideas here:
....

Wednesday:
Forget and *focus* on the song 'Be still' – track 10 – from the CD; you will find the words on page 60. Play it several times. *Fink* and write any *follow*-through ideas here: ....
....

Thursday:
Forget and *focus* on the poem 'You!' on page 60. Scan it over slowly and *fink*. Write any *follow*-through ideas here: ....
....

Friday:
Forget and *focus* on Luke 18:35–43, where Jesus heals the blind man. Read it several times, slowly. Imagine you were the blind man; how do you feel about meeting Jesus? *Focus* and write any *follow*-through ideas here: ....
....
....

Saturday:
Light a candle and turn out the lights in your prayer site (get permission first, if necessary). *Forget* and *focus* on the flame. *Fink* and write any *follow*-through ideas here: ....
....
....

prayer *log*

[YOU WRITE DATE]

I LISTENED TO GOD

DAYS OF THE WEEK

WEEK STARTING SUNDAY:

I PRAYED FOR OTHERS

SUN
MON
TUES
WED
THUR
FRI
SAT

web site

I WORSHIPPED

I PRAYED FOR MYSELF

I SAID SORRY

I SAID THANKS

prayer log II web site

Instructions for this week are found on pages 56 and 57.

As you take time out to listen to God you may feel that he is telling you to do something (eg write to an old friend, make up a broken relationship or get involved in your youth group – it could be anything!). Make a note of any *Follow*-through Action Points here: ....

....

....

....

....

....

....

....

Letting
God speak

Try repeating these short one-line prayers as a way of *forgetting* everything except that Jesus is with you:

'Jesus, thank you for coming here.'

'Speak Lord; I want to hear your voice.'

'Lighten my darkness, Lord, I pray.'

prayer file 6

BE STILL

Be still, for the presence of the Lord, the Holy One is here.
Come bow before Him now with reverence and fear.
In Him no sin is found, we stand on holy ground;
Be still for the presence of the Lord, the Holy One is here.

Be still, for the glory of the Lord is shining all around.
He burns with holy fire, with splendour He is crowned.
How awesome is the sight, our radiant King of light;
Be still, for the glory of the Lord is shining all around.

Be still for the power of the Lord is moving in this place.
He comes to cleanse and heal, to minister his grace.
No work too hard for Him, in faith receive from Him;
Be still, for the power of the Lord is moving in this place.

Dave Evans© 1986 Kingsway's Thank You Music

YOU!

Where I wander – You!
Where I ponder – You again, always You!
You! You! You!
When I am gladdened – You!
When I am saddened – You!
Only You. You again, always You!
You! You! You!
You above! You below!
In every trend, at every end.
Only You. You again, always You!
You! You! You!

Levi Yitzchak of Beritchev, from Another Day – Prayers of the Human Family edited by John Carden, published by Triangle 1986. Copyright © 1986 Triangle. Used with permission.

You're on your own now!

Well done! You have completed eleven weeks of prayer training! You have learned how to e-x-p-a-n-d your prayer life by

Worshipping – saying sorry – saying thanks – praying for yourself – praying for others – letting God speak.

From now on it's up to you to continue covering those six prayer areas on your own. You have got this book and CD to use as a resource so keep referring back to it to refresh your memory.

On the following pages we have given you two more weeks' *Prayer Logs* and *Prayer Webs* to get you started (p64,66).

On the next two pages we have also given you the low-down on making your own *Prayer Wall-planner*. A lot of people use similar visual aids to help them pray – so why not join them!

What To Do Each Day

weeks 12+13 (to eternity)

1 Using all of the ideas from this book, your newly-created *Prayer Wall-planner* (and any resources you have come across), make an attempt to: worship, say sorry, say thanks, pray for yourself, pray for others and listen to God each day.

2 Mark the *Prayer Webs* to show how you are doing. If you fail to pray one day, don't feel anxious and don't give up. Every day is a new start as far as God is concerned!

3 Make a note of any answered prayers in the box in the bottom right hand corner of the page.

4 Use the spaces in the *Prayer Logs* both to jot down things to pray about during the day, and to note down thoughts or actions that God brings to mind as you pray.

make your own Prayer wall-planner

1 Get hold of a cork notice-board from your local hardware shop or DIY superstore.

2 Divide the board into six sections with strips of coloured paper, tape or ribbon.

3 On six postcard-sized pieces of card write the chapter headings from this book:

> God – you're awesome
> Come clean
> Cool, God!
> Dear God – help!
> Standing in the gap
> Time out

4 Over the coming weeks, collect pictures, photos, song lyrics, Bible verses etc which will help you pray in each section. For example:

● in the *God – you're awesome* section you could put pictures of a part of creation, say a volcano, to remind you of God's power; or you could write out words from a favourite worship song.

● in the *Come clean* section you could place a picture of Jesus on the cross to remind you of the cost of your forgiveness.

● in the *Cool, God!* section you could create your own 'thanks' collage similar to that on page 34.

● in the *Standing in the gap* section you could put photos of your family, your youth group leaders or church missionaries together with a map of the 10/40 window (see pages 36 and 68).

5 When it's complete, fix the notice-board somewhere in your prayer space and use it to inspire your daily prayer times.

God – you're awesome

Cool, God!

Come clean

Dear God – help!

Standing in the gap

Time out

TIP: About once a term have a change around to prevent you getting too familiar with your *Prayer Wall-planner;* pin up some new pictures and get hold of some new up-to-date photos.

prayer log

Pray at all times, be thankful in all circumstances. This is what God wants from you...

1 Thessalonians 5:17,18

Sunday:

Monday:

Tuesday:

Wednesday:

Thursday:

Friday:

Saturday:

WEEK STARTING SUNDAY:

[YOU WRITE DATE]

I LISTENED TO GOD

I PRAYED FOR OTHERS

DAYS OF THE WEEK

SUN
MON
TUES
WED
THUR
FRI
SAT

web site

I WORSHIPPED

I PRAYED FOR MYSELF

I SAID THANKS

I SAID SORRY

prayer log 12 web site

DEALING WITH WANDERING THOUGHTS
When you start to pray, your mind may well fill up with all kinds of thoughts and ideas that are nothing to do with what you wanted to pray about: 'Did we have science homework tonight?' 'Is the video set for the big match?' 'Will Sophie lend me her hockey stick for the weekend?' etc!
Keep a piece of paper next to you so that you can scribble down any distracting thoughts to follow up later. Once you've written them down, you can leave them to deal with later and get back to your prayers.

If you suddenly realise that your mind has been wandering for quite a while, you have lost concentration in a BIG way! Stand up, jump up and down 10 times, then get straight back into your next prayer. (No, it's not in the Bible, but it might help!)

Ask, and you *will* receive; seek, and you *will* find; knock, and the door *will* be opened to you.

Matthew 7:7

Sunday:

....
....
....

Monday:

....
....
....

Tuesday:

....
....
....

Wednesday:

....
....
....

Thursday:

....
....
....

Friday:

....
....
....

Saturday:

....
....
....

prayer*log*

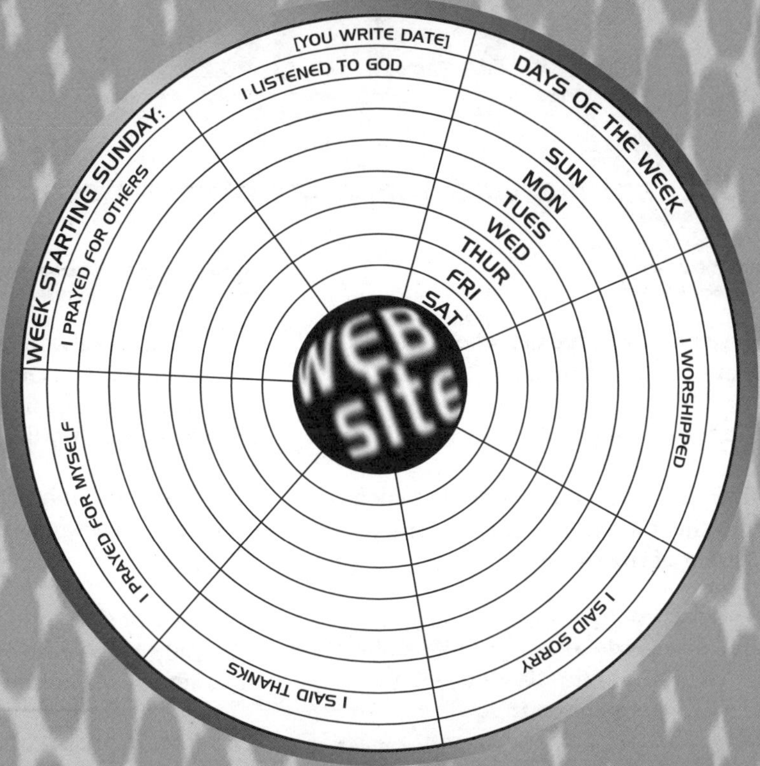
[YOU WRITE DATE]
WEEK STARTING SUNDAY:
DAYS OF THE WEEK
SUN
MON
TUES
WED
THUR
FRI
SAT
I LISTENED TO GOD
I PRAYED FOR OTHERS
I PRAYED FOR MYSELF
I SAID THANKS
I SAID SORRY
I WORSHIPPED
WEB site

prayer log 13 web site

WELCOME JESUS

If praying to God in 'heaven' makes God feel a long way away, put a spare chair in your prayer space, close your eyes and imagine that Jesus has come into the room and is sitting on the chair listening to your prayers.

Standing in the gap
REVISITED

[asking God for what others need]

- Jesus died to save the *whole* world, not just Great Britain.

- God loves *all* people of every nation.

- The church is supposed to be taking the Good News of Jesus into *every* corner of the world.

Dig out your world atlas and write some of the countries in the 10/40 window here: (see map on page 36)

....
....
....
....
....
....
....
....
....
....
....
....
....
....
....
....
....
....

Pray for them regularly. Ask God to help Christians who live there to be kept safe from harm and to be able to tell people about Jesus.

Did you also know?

- 42% of the world's population cannot find a church of their own language and culture near to where they live.

- Christians only give 0.1% of their income to reach these people.

- 20% of the world is Muslim but only 2% of missionaries are sent to Muslim countries.

- 97% of people of the least evangelised countries live in the area highlighted on the map on page 36 (this area is called the 10/40 window because of the lines of latitude and longitude that mark its borders).

- 2.7 billion Muslims, Buddhists and Hindus live in the 10/40 window.

- 82% of the poorest people in the world live in the 10/40 window.

- We need to pray especially hard for the people who live in the 10/40 window and for the missionaries who are trying to reach them with the good news of Jesus.